NATIONAL PARKS

EVERGLADES
NATIONAL PARK

by Maddie Spalding

Content Consultant
Harold R. Wanless, PhD
Department of Geological Sciences
University of Miami

Core Library

An Imprint of Abdo Publishing
abdopublishing.com

abdopublishing.com

Published by Abdo Publishing, a division of ABDO, PO Box 398166, Minneapolis, Minnesota 55439. Copyright © 2017 by Abdo Consulting Group, Inc. International copyrights reserved in all countries. No part of this book may be reproduced in any form without written permission from the publisher. Core Library™ is a trademark and logo of Abdo Publishing.

Printed in the United States of America, North Mankato, Minnesota
072016
012017

THIS BOOK CONTAINS
RECYCLED MATERIALS

Cover Photo: Yin Yang/iStockphoto
Interior Photos: Yin Yang/iStockphoto, 1; Don Fink/Shutterstock Images, 4; Library of Congress, 7; Rudy Umans/Shutterstock Images, 10; Everglades National Park Service, 12, 39, 45; William Silver/Shutterstock Images, 15; Jo Crebbin/Shutterstock Images, 18; Shutterstock Images, 22 (deer); Eric Isselee/Shutterstock Images, 22 (raccoon), 22 (fox); iStockphoto, 22 (opossum), 23; CLS Design/Shutterstock Images, 22 (rabbit); Bob Eastman/iStockphoto, 22 (bobcat); North Wind Picture Archives, 26, 29, 32; View Apart/Shutterstock Images, 34; Kevin Derrick/iStockphoto, 38; EvergladesRestoration.gov, 41; National Park Service, 42–43

Editor: Mirella Miller
Series Designer: Ryan Gale

Publisher's Cataloging-in-Publication Data

Names: Spalding, Maddie, author.
Title: Everglades National Park / by Maddie Spalding.
Description: Minneapolis, MN : Abdo Publishing, 2017. | Series: National parks
    | Includes bibliographical references and index.
Identifiers: LCCN 2016945458 | ISBN 9781680784718 (lib. bdg.) |
    ISBN 9781680798562 (ebook)
Subjects: LCSH: Everglades National Park (Fla.)--Juvenile literature.
Classification: DDC 975.9/39--dc23
LC record available at http://lccn.loc.gov/2016945458

CONTENTS

A RIVER OF GRASS

The midmorning sun glints on the water. The park ranger lifts one booted foot and steps into the swampy Shark River Slough. Her tour group follows. Small fish dart through the water. Tall cypress trees rise from the marsh. A white heron watches the group. Tall sawgrass hugs the trees. The group follows their guide farther into the waist-deep swamps of Everglades National Park.

A variety of habitats are found in Everglades National Park.

Everglades National Park stretches across 1.5 million acres (607,000 ha). It is located at the southernmost tip of the Florida peninsula. The park's environment is unlike any other national park. This is because it is close to the equator. Much of the park is made up of everglades, or swampy grasslands. Prairies, woodlands, and islands can also be found here. Many animals and plants thrive in this warm and wet climate.

A World Heritage Site

Everglades National Park became a World Heritage Site on October 26, 1979. The United Nations Educational, Scientific and Cultural Organization (UNESCO) chooses World Heritage Sites. The site must benefit the community and the world as a whole. Everglades National Park was nominated and chosen because of its diverse habitats and wildlife. UNESCO also recognized it as a park that protects many threatened animal species.

Preserving Florida's Wetlands

Everglades settlers in the late 1800s and early 1900s saw the wetlands as an inconvenience. They could not farm land that was

Workers dug the Miami Canal in the 1920s.

underwater. They also could not build houses or roads on this landscape. So they began digging canals. A canal is a long and narrow passageway. Water from the marshes flowed into these canals. It drained south into the Atlantic Ocean. Settlers turned the northern Everglades into sugarcane plantations, cattle ranches, and vegetable fields.

Ernest Coe was one of the first to speak up against land development in the Everglades. Coe was a landscape architect. He was shocked to learn about habitat loss in the Everglades. He formed the Tropical Everglades National Park Association in 1928. This organization fought for the creation of a national park in south Florida.

Coe enlisted the help of writer Marjory Stoneman Douglas. Douglas visited the area in the 1920s. Her observations later led her to write a book called *The Everglades: River of Grass*. It was published in November 1947. Readers were excited by Douglas's descriptions of the Everglades' scenery and landscapes.

PERSPECTIVES
Truman's Speech

President Harry S. Truman gave a speech during the opening of Everglades National Park. He described why the area needed to be preserved:

This Everglades area has more than its share of features unique to these United States. . . . Here is land, tranquil in its quiet beauty, serving not as the source of water but as the last receiver of it. To its natural abundance we owe the spectacular plant and animal life that distinguishes this place from all others in the country.

The Park's Beginnings

Everglades National Park opened on December 6, 1947. Coe and Douglas's efforts had helped convince the public that the Everglades were worth saving. But the fight for the park's creation had been a long battle.

Activists helped the public discover the Everglades' natural beauty. They helped protect a land that might have been ignored or destroyed. Now many people travel to the Everglades. This "river of grass" contains many plants and wildlife that cannot be found anywhere else in the world.

EXPLORE ONLINE

Chapter One talks about key features of Everglades National Park. The website below goes into more depth about this topic. How is the information from the website the same as the information in Chapter One? What new information did you learn from the website?

Everglades National Park
mycorelibrary.com/everglades

CHAPTER TWO

GEOLOGICAL HISTORY

The Everglades National Park landscape that visitors see now was very different approximately 200 million years ago. Earth's continents were then joined together as one. Scientists call this continent Pangaea. When Pangaea shifted and broke apart, part of the African plate remained attached to North America. This landmass

A layer of limestone forms the foundation of the Florida Platform.

Water that soaks into the soil and limestone in the
Everglades allows wetland plants to grow.

was the Florida Platform. The Florida Platform
became the foundation of present-day Florida.

Then the climate warmed approximately
65 million years ago. Glaciers in the northern parts
of North America began to melt. This caused the sea
levels to rise. The Florida Platform was sunken in a
shallow sea. Sea creatures such as shellfish sank to
the ocean floor after they died. Their shells began
forming a layer of limestone on top of the Florida

Platform. Limestone is a hard white rock.

The Florida peninsula emerged from the water approximately 23 million years ago as sea levels fell. Sand and clay deposits covered the limestone. Acidic rainwater dissolved some of the limestone, creating small cracks in the rock. Pits also formed in the rock. Water seeped into these open spaces. This process formed the Biscayne Aquifer approximately 110,000 years ago. The Biscayne Aquifer lies underneath the soil in southeast Florida. It allows the Everglades to store freshwater.

Prescribed Fires

Lightning occurs more often in Florida than in any other US state. Lightning can strike dry grass and start a wildfire. Wildfires help maintain the marshland and other habitats in the Everglades. But wildfires can spread quickly and become out of control. Everglades National Park workers use prescribed fires to keep flames within the park boundaries. Prescribed fires are planned and controlled carefully. Workers make sure the fires burn slowly so animals have enough time to move to a safe place.

A Varied Landscape

The Great Ice Age that began approximately
2.6 million years ago formed much of Everglades
National Park's landscape. The Great Ice Age
consisted of many shorter ice ages. Glacial freshwater
fed into seas and made sea levels rise during warming
periods. Sea levels fell during cold periods when polar
ice sheets grew in size. The sea around south Florida
deposited sediments. The constant movement of the
sea shaped these sediments into landforms.

The Atlantic Coastal Ridge forms a rim along the
park's southeast edge. It ranges in elevation from
5 to 20 feet (2 to 6 m) above sea level. This ridge
keeps water in the Everglades from flowing east into
the Atlantic Ocean. Water flows southwest instead.

Sediment deposits also formed islands along the
west coast of Florida in the Gulf of Mexico. These
islands make up the Ten Thousand Islands area.
Mangrove trees grow in the shallow waters off the
coast. Over time the sea deposited sand and silt in

The Florida coast is home to many mangrove trees.

the roots of these trees. These deposits gradually
built up into islands.

Wetland Formation

South Florida has a subtropical climate. The area is
dry in the winter but humid in the summer. Rainstorms
are common in the summer. As much as 24 inches
(61 cm) of rain can fall on the area in one day.

PERSPECTIVES
Wetland Restoration

Water flow into the Everglades has been reduced since the 1880s, when settlers began building canals in the wetlands. Workers also built a highway called the Tamiami Trail through the Everglades in 1915. This road blocked water flow south from Lake Okeechobee. Hydrologist Bob Johnson remains hopeful that much of this water flow can be restored. He measures water levels in the Everglades, which have risen since parts of the road were removed. He predicts: "You'll see very slow flow through the marsh back the way it's supposed to be: the river of grass."

Lake Okeechobee formed along the northern edge of the Everglades after a warming period. This lake overflows in the summer. The freshwater flows 100 miles (161 km) through the Everglades until it reaches Florida Bay and the Gulf of Mexico. This water flow and the heavy summer rainstorms helped create the wetland landscape that Everglades National Park visitors see now.

Writer Marjory Stoneman Douglas admired the Everglades landscape in her book *The Everglades: River of Grass*. She wrote:

> *There are no other Everglades in the world. They are, they have always been, one of the unique regions of the earth, remote, never wholly known. Nothing anywhere else is like them: their vast glittering openness, wider than the enormous visible round of the horizon, the racing free saltness and sweetness of their massive winds, under the dazzling blue heights of space. They are unique also in the simplicity, the diversity, the related harmony of the forms of life they enclose. The miracle of the light pours over the green and brown expanse of saw grass and of water, shining and slow-moving below, the grass and water that is the meaning and the central fact of the Everglades of Florida. It is a river of grass.*

Source: Marjory Stoneman Douglas. The Everglades: River of Grass. Sarasota, FL: Pineapple Press, 2007. Print. 5–6.

Consider Your Audience

Adapt this passage for a different audience, such as a teacher or a friend. Write a blog post conveying this same information to the new audience. How does your post differ from the original text, and why?

BIOLOGICAL HISTORY

All wilderness areas have a biological history. This is the history of all the plant and animal life that has existed in the area. Everglades National Park has a rich biological history. The subtropical climate of South America and the temperate North American climate merge in the park. These two climates support different kinds of plants and animals. Freshwater and saltwater habitats also

The Florida panther is Florida's official state animal and can be seen in the Everglades.

Endangered Plants and Animals

The Everglades is home to 20 species of endangered animals and 59 species of endangered plants. Some orchid species became endangered when poachers took them from their habitats. Poaching also endangered some animals. The Florida panther is the park's most endangered animal. Poachers hunted these panthers in the mid-1800s. Invasive species are another threat. These are species that are not native to the park. They invade habitats and harm native species. This can disrupt the balance of the ecosystem. One common invasive animal is the Burmese python. These snakes can kill animals as big as alligators.

support a variety of plants and animals.

Prehistoric Animals

Many prehistoric animals once lived in Florida. Archaeologists have found the bones of extinct animals. Some of the fish and bird fossils they found are approximately 50 million years old. Megalodon teeth have been found throughout Florida. These were giant sharks that are estimated to have been up to 50 feet (15 m) long.

Most of Florida's large prehistoric animals

roamed the area between 10,000 and 25,000 years ago. Archaeologists have found bones from giant sloths that stood up to 18 feet (5 m) tall. Wooly mammoths lived in the area until they became extinct approximately 13,000 years ago. Other ancient animals in south Florida included camels with long necks resembling giraffes.

Today's Animals

Everglades National Park visitors will not encounter mammoths or giant sloths. But a wide variety of animals can still be found. Many people come to see crocodiles and alligators. South Florida is the only place in the world where American crocodiles and American alligators coexist. The American alligator lives throughout the southeastern United States. The American crocodile lives mostly in South America but also inhabits parts of south Florida. Crocodiles can live in saltwater and freshwater habitats. Alligators live mainly in freshwater. Florida Bay, located at the southernmost part of the park, is an ideal habitat

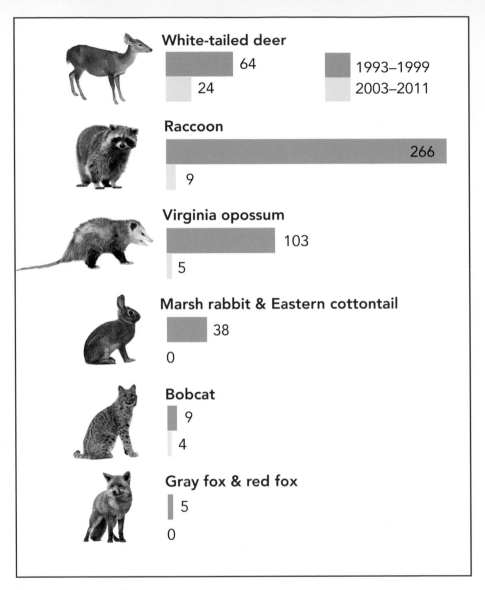

White-tailed deer
- 64
- 24

■ 1993–1999
□ 2003–2011

Raccoon
- 266
- 9

Virginia opossum
- 103
- 5

Marsh rabbit & Eastern cottontail
- 38
- 0

Bobcat
- 9
- 4

Gray fox & red fox
- 5
- 0

Mammal Decline

Invasive animal species such as the Burmese python have shrunk some of the mammal populations in Everglades National Park. The diagram above shows mammal populations in the park recorded between 1993 and 1999. It also shows mammal populations recorded between 2003 and 2011. What differences do you notice between these populations?

American alligators bask in the sun in Everglades National Park.

for both alligators and crocodiles. Here, freshwater from swamps combines with saltwater from the Gulf of Mexico.

The warm and shallow wetland environment attracts many birds. More than 360 species of birds live in the park. Wading birds such as herons have long legs that are suited to watery habitats. They stand in the marshes and dip their bills in the water to catch fish.

A Variety of Vegetation

Each of Everglades National Park's habitats has its own unique plant life. One common habitat is a hardwood hammock. A hardwood hammock is a cluster of trees that grows in areas of raised elevation. Tropical plants such as cocoplum trees grow in these hammocks. They have small white fruit that wildlife often eats. Temperate plants such as oak and maple trees also grow in these hammocks.

Mangrove forests grow near the coast of

Florida Bay. Mangrove trees thrive in both freshwater and saltwater environments. These trees protect the mainland from hurricanes. Their tangled roots grow deep into the soil. These roots anchor the trees to the ground during storms. This wall of trees keeps the worst of the storms from moving inland.

The Everglades also has more species of orchids than any other US national park. Orchids are plants that produce colorful flowers. Orchids flourish in the wetlands and hardwood hammocks.

FURTHER EVIDENCE

Chapter Three introduced you to some plant and animal species that live in Everglades National Park. What was one of the main points of this chapter? What evidence is included to support this point? Read the article at the website below. Find a quote from the website that supports the chapter's main point.

Everglades Wildlife
mycorelibrary.com/everglades

CHAPTER FOUR

EARLY SETTLEMENT IN THE EVERGLADES

The Everglades' wetland environment may not seem like a place that could support much human life. But 12,000 years ago, south Florida was much cooler and drier than it is today. The area's first inhabitants likely lived in the area around this time. These were the Paleo-Indian people. Historians believed the Paleo-Indian people shared the land with animals such as mammoths and bison. They hunted

Paleo-Indians living in the Everglades area hunted for their food.

Prehistoric Trash Piles

Hundreds of tree islands rise up from the wetlands in Everglades National Park. Scientists were curious about how these piles formed. They dug at the base of some of the islands to find out. They found reddish-grey cemented layers underneath the soil. These layers were up to 30 inches (75 cm) thick. They were made up of animal bones, seeds, and other human artifacts. Scientists estimate these items are approximately 4,000 years old.

these animals for food. They later hunted deer, rabbits, and fish when the wetlands began to form.

Spanish Explorers Arrive

The Paleo-Indian people were likely the ancestors of some of the tribes that later lived in south Florida. Approximately 20,000 people lived in the area when the first Spanish explorers landed in 1513. The Spanish encountered at least five tribes. The Tequesta tribe lived south of the Everglades. The Jeaga and Ais tribes lived along the east coast. The Mayaimi tribe lived in central Florida, near Lake Okeechobee.

The Spanish explorers disrupted the American Indians' way of life by bringing disease and starting wars.

The Calusa tribe was spread out across southwest Florida. They survived in the wetlands by building their houses on stilts.

Spanish explorers carried diseases such as smallpox. The native people had never faced these diseases before. Many died. Others were killed in wars with the Spanish. Still others were forced into slavery. The English gained control of Florida in 1763. By that time, the native population had declined to several hundred. Some of these people remained in the Everglades. Others migrated south to Cuba.

A Wetland Refuge

Europeans continued to settle North America in the early 1800s. Many pushed native people from their homelands. US general Andrew Jackson led a war against the Creek tribe in 1813. The Creek tribe lived in present-day Georgia and Alabama. Jackson's troops defeated the Creek people, forcing them to give up most of their lands. Some survivors fled south to Florida. The Creek Nation then split into two tribes: the Miccosukees and the Seminoles.

In the early 1800s, slavery was legal in the United States. Hundreds of black runaway slaves took refuge in Florida. These slaves lived alongside the Seminoles and Miccosukees. These tribes offered runaway slaves protection. This angered Southern slave owners and government officials.

The US Army invaded Florida in 1817. It wanted to return slaves to their owners. It also wanted to open up Florida to US settlement. Jackson and his troops burned American Indian towns and recaptured runaway slaves.

Jackson became president in 1829. He passed the Indian Removal Act one year later. This act allowed him to relocate tribes to reservations west of the Mississippi River. But many American Indians refused to leave their lands. They sought refuge in the Everglades. US troops again invaded the area.

PERSPECTIVES
Modern Everglades Tribal Life

Approximately 4,400 Seminole and Miccosukee people now live in Florida. They live in reservations around Everglades National Park. Some American Indians who live near the Everglades continue to hold on to old traditions such as wearing tribal beads. But many have adopted a more modern way of living. This transition began in 1947, when park rules outlawed hunting and fishing. The Seminole and Miccosukee people were forced to give up their former way of life.

The Seminoles built homes in the safety of the Everglades in the 1800s.

They captured a key Seminole leader. Many Seminoles then agreed to relocate. By 1858 only approximately 300 American Indians remained in Florida.

The Everglades area has important historical significance to Colley Billie, former Chairman of the Miccosukee Tribe of Indians of Florida. He said:

> During the Indian removal of the early to mid-1800s, when Indian tribes were being forced to move west into present-day Oklahoma and Kansas, our tribal members sought refuge in the remote Florida Everglades. We went from a dry land environment to subtropical wetland—an area that is mostly water. Although this new land was vastly different from any territory our people had ever encountered, we were able not only to adapt, but also eventually to thrive in this novel environment.
>
> This is a reflection of the versatility and adaptability of the Miccosukee people to thrive in the face of adversity and turn hardship into opportunity.

Source: "Meet Native America: Colley Billie, Chairman of the Miccosukee Tribe of Indians in Florida." National Museum of the American Indian. *Smithsonian Institution,* February 28, 2014. Web. Accessed April 21, 2016.

Back It Up

The speaker in this passage is using evidence to support a point. Write a paragraph describing the point the speaker is making. Then write down two or three pieces of evidence he uses to make his point.

CHAPTER FIVE

EVERGLADES NATIONAL PARK TODAY

More than 1 million people visit Everglades National Park each year. Some come to explore sloughs. Some come to catch a glimpse of wading birds or wetland reptiles. Many are drawn to Everglades National Park simply because its environment is so different from any other US national park.

Groups of visitors enjoy airboat rides through the park.

Climate Change

President Barack Obama visited the Everglades in April 2015. He used the Everglades as an example of why the government needed to take action on climate change. Sea levels around the Everglades have risen as Earth warms. Saltwater from the ocean flows inland. This can harm freshwater wildlife. Obama suggested that reducing pollution can stop some of this damage.

Park Attractions

The park has many entrances. Visitors can enter through the Gulf Coast Visitor Center. Just past this entrance, they can boat through the Ten Thousand Islands. The Shark Valley Visitor Center is another entrance. It is located in the heart of the Everglades. Visitors will not find sharks in Shark Valley. But they will probably see alligators sunning themselves along hiking paths. The southernmost visitor entrance is near the Flamingo Visitor Center. Visitors might see flamingos in this area.

Visitors who do not mind getting their feet wet can go slough slogging. Everglades National Park has two main sloughs. Shark River Slough extends from the northeast corner of the park. Taylor Slough is located along the park's southeast edge. Park rangers guide groups through sloughs, where they can admire cypress tress and other wetland plants up close.

Visitors can also explore by canoe. Nine Mile Pond is one of the most popular canoe trails. Cocoplum trees rise up from tree islands in this pond. Turner River in the northwest corner of the park is

PERSPECTIVES
Oil Drilling Near the Everglades

While oil drilling is not allowed in Everglades National Park, it is allowed in Big Cypress National Preserve. This preserve is located next to the Everglades. The National Park Service (NPS) believes oil drilling will have only a small impact on endangered wildlife. However, some environmentalists disagree. Matthew Schwartz is part of the South Florida Wildlands Association. He believes female Florida panthers may abandon their dens while the nearby drilling is going on. He has asked the NPS to do more studies in the area before they approve the operations.

Manatees are protected by the government.

another popular canoe trail. Canoers here might spot manatees swimming near the shore of the Gulf of Mexico. Experienced canoers can explore the 99-mile (159-km) Wilderness Waterway. This waterway of interconnected bays stretches from Everglades City to the Flamingo Visitor Center.

The Comprehensive Everglades Restoration Plan

The Everglades once covered more than 4,000 square miles (10,360 sq km). But this region is now less than

Updating the dams, levees, and trails in the Everglades will eventually lead to increased water flow.

half of its original size. Land development and canal construction in the 1800s drained much of these wetlands. The US government also built more canals in 1947 to protect Florida against hurricanes. These canals reduced water flow into the Everglades.

The Florida government and the federal government are committed to restoring some of these wetlands. They have partnered to work on the largest environmental restoration project in US history. This is the Comprehensive Everglades Restoration Plan (CERP).

Congress approved the CERP in 2000. The CERP consists of more than 60 projects. These are all meant to increase the flow of freshwater into the Everglades. They also restore freshwater habitats for animals such as alligators. Workers have removed many canals and dams. They have also removed parts of the Tamiami Trail. They have built bridges to replace these sections of the trail. Freshwater can flow south underneath these bridges into the Everglades.

These projects have increased water flow into the Everglades. But there is still a long way to go. The National Park Service (NPS) estimates it will take more than 30 years to complete the CERP. Increasing freshwater flow in the wetlands is a slow process. The water has to be released in the right quantities and areas. Though it will take many years, this project will go a long way toward restoring the river of grass.

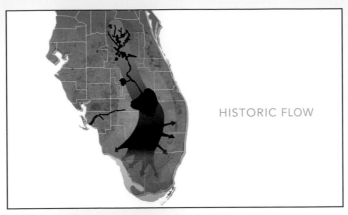

HISTORIC FLOW

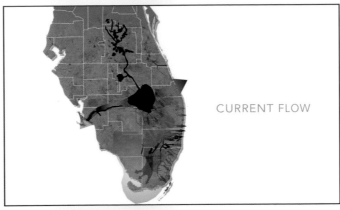

CURRENT FLOW

RESTORED FLOW

Water Flow in the Everglades

Compare the above images. How has water flow in the Everglades changed over time? How will the Comprehensive Everglades Restoration Plan redirect water flow?

PARK MAP

Gulf Coast
Visitor Center

Turner River
Canoe Trail

Tamiami Trail

Ten Thousand Islands

Wilderness Waterway

GULF OF MEXICO

Nine Mile
Pond

Flamingo Visitor Center

North | 0   5   10 Kilometers
↑ | 0   5   10 Miles

Shark Valley Visitor Center

Shark River Slough

Taylor Slough

Florida Bay

ATLANTIC OCEAN

STOP AND THINK

Take a Stand

Miccosukee and Seminole ancestors lived off the land for thousands of years. But they are no longer allowed to hunt or fish in the area. Some feel as though they have been cut off from their homeland. Do you think they should be allowed to hunt and fish in the park? Why or why not? What could be done to preserve both the Everglades and native traditions?

Another View

This book talks about oil drilling operations near Everglades National Park. As you know, every source is different. Ask a librarian or another adult to help you find another source about this subject. Write a short essay comparing and contrasting the new source's point of view with that of this book's author. What is the point of view of each author? How are they similar and why? How are they different and why?

Why Do I Care?

Maybe you do not have a national park near you. But that doesn't mean you can't think about how national parks are important. How do national parks affect your life? Do you have friends or family who have worked in a national park? How might life be different if there were no national parks?

You Are There

Imagine you are among the first people to settle in the Everglades. Write a letter home. What do you notice about the landscape? What plants and animals can you find? Be sure to add plenty of details.

GLOSSARY

aquifer
a layer of rock or sand that can hold water

peninsula
a piece of land that sticks out from a larger landmass and is almost completely surrounded by water

plate
one of the sheets of rock that make up Earth's outer crust

poacher
a person who hunts or fishes illegally on someone else's land

refuge
a place that provides protection or shelter

reservation
an area of land set aside by the government for a specific purpose

sediment
rock, sand, or dirt that has been carried to a place by water, wind, or a glacier

silt
sand, soil, or mud that is carried by flowing water and then sinks

slough
a low-lying area of land that channels water through wetlands

temperate
having neither very hot nor very cold temperatures

LEARN MORE

Books

Furstinger, Nancy. *The Everglades: The Largest Marsh in the United States.* New York: AV2, 2014.

Marsico, Katie. *The Everglades.* Ann Arbor, MI: Cherry Lake, 2013.

Mattern, Joanne. *Marjory Stoneman Douglas.* Minneapolis, MN: Abdo, 2014.

Websites

To learn more about National Parks, visit **booklinks.abdopublishing.com**. These links are routinely monitored and updated to provide the most current information available.

Visit **mycorelibrary.com** for free additional tools for teachers and students.

INDEX

ABOUT THE AUTHOR

Maddie Spalding is a writer from Minnesota. She enjoys writing about history and the environment. She has visited a few US national parks and hopes to visit more in the future.